NEA:
The Grab for Power

A Chronology of the
National Education Association

All Scripture quotations are from the King James Version of the Holy Bible.

Printed in the United States of America

ISBN 1-57558-52-7

NEA:
The Grab for Power

A Chronology of the
National Education Association

Dennis L. Cuddy

Table of Contents

Introduction

Most of the problems in America today can be traced to the on-going battle between the principles of the American and French revolutions. The American Revolution was based largely upon principles of biblical morality, capitalism, and individual responsibility. The watchwords of the French Revolution were "liberty, equality, fraternity," which at first sound quite commendable. However, by *liberty* was meant license, a "do-your-own-thing" morality rebelling against authority. By *equality* was not meant equal opportunity, but rather a leveling of the masses under "philosopher-kings," an elite (including educational) who through social engineering would shape a socialistic society. And by *fraternity* was not meant a brotherhood based upon the Holy Bible, but rather a humanistic brotherhood based upon what all ethical systems have in common.

That humanistic education is "religious" proselytizing of students in opposition to biblical beliefs is evident from a statement by John Dewey, co-author of the first Humanist Manifesto (1933) and honorary National Education Association (NEA) president (1932) in "Religion and Our Schools" (*The Hibbert Journal,* July 1908):

> Our schools . . . are performing an infinitely religious work. They are promoting the social unity out of which in the end genuine religious unity must grow. . . . Religion . . . associated with . . . dogmatic beliefs . . . we see . . . disappearing. . . . It is the part of man to labor persistently and patiently for the clarification and development of the positive creed of life . . . , and to work for the transformation of all practical instrumentalities of education till they are in harmony with these ideas.

The non-dogmatic "positive creed of life" which Dewey would come to call a "common faith" was like the humanistic brotherhood (and sisterhood) of the French Revolution. And the NEA has been perhaps the organization most responsible for furthering the principles of the French Revolution in the United States in this century. The following chronology of this labor union during this time is not meant to be complete, but rather simply to identify important events, people, and quotations relating to this powerful and politically ambitious organization.

Chronology

1906

- *June 30:* The National Education Association (NEA) becomes federally chartered or incorporated (H.R. 10501, Public No. 398). The NEA had been founded in 1857, but until 1870 was called the National Teachers Association.

1912

- The NEA begins to promote the training of teachers in sex education and sex hygiene.

1913

- The NEA establishes the Commission on the Reorganization of Secondary Education, which has a membership including several "young rebels" of the era. The commission will produce a report in 1918 containing seven cardinal principles or objectives for the education of every American boy and girl, including "ethical character."

- The NEA issues Bulletin 41, which states:

  It is not so important that the pupil know how the President is elected or that he shall understand the duties of the health officer in his community. The time formerly spent in the effort to understand the process of passing a law under the President's veto is now to be more preferably used in the observation of vocational resources of the community. The committee recommends that social studies in the high school shall include community health, housing, homes, human rights versus property rights, . . . the selfish conservatism of traditions and public utilities.

1915

- The "Educational Trust," known as the Cleveland Group (because its first meeting is in Cleveland), meets for the first time. Among the members of the group are: George Strayer, professor at Teachers College and NEA president 1918–19; Elwood Cubberly, dean of Stanford University's School of Education; and leader of the "Educational Trust," Charles Judd (colleague of John Dewey), who received his Ph.D. from Wilhelm Wundt in Leipzig in 1896.

In David Tyack and Elisabeth Hansot's *Managers of Virtue* (1982), Judd is quoted as urging the Cleveland conference to attempt "the positive and aggressive task of . . . a detailed reorganization of the materials of instruction in schools of all grades. . . ." Tyack and Hansot will also write:

There were "placement barons," usually professors of educational administration in universities such as Teachers College, Harvard, University of Chicago, or Stanford, who had an inside track in placing their graduates in important positions. One educator commented after spending a weekend with Cubberly in Palo Alto that "Cubberly had an educational Tammany Hall that made the Strayer-Engelhardt Tammany Hall in New York look very weak." . . . [And] one principal recalled "Strayer's Law" for dealing with disloyal subordinates is "Give 'em the axe."

This is the beginning of a plan to use the "credentialing process" to control education.

1929

▪ *October 19:* The NEA presents John Dewey, "Father of Progressive Education," with a "Life Membership." As *NEA Journal* editor Joy Elmer Morgan says, it is ". . . for the ideas which you have set afloat upon the sea of human thought . . ." (see *NEA Journal,* December 1929).

This is the same year in which Dewey authors *Individualism, Old and New,* in which he proclaims: "We are in for some kind of socialism, call it by whatever name we please, and no matter what it will be called when it is realized. . . ."

And this is the year after Dewey has written a glowing article about the Russian schools, having just returned from the Soviet Union. In the December 5, 1928, edition of *The New Republic,* Dewey described

> . . . the marvelous development of progressive educational ideas and practices under the fostering care of the Bolshevist government . . . the required collective and cooperative mentality. . . . The great task of the school is to counteract and transform those domestic and neighborhood tendencies . . . the influence of home and Church. . . .

1932

▪ John Dewey is made honorary president of the NEA, and in 1933 will co-author the first *Humanist Manifesto.* In 1934 Dewey will author *A Common Faith,* in which he proclaims:

> It is impossible to ignore the fact that historic Christianity has been committed to a separation of sheep and goats; the saved and the lost; the elect and the mass. . . . Those outside the fold of the church and those who do not rely upon belief in the supernatural have been regarded as only potential brothers, still requiring adoption into the family. I cannot understand how any realization of the democratic ideal as a vital moral and spiritual ideal in human affairs is possible without surrender of the conception of the basic division to which supernatural Christianity is committed.

1934

▪ *July:* At the seventy-second annual meeting of the NEA held in Washington, D.C., in a report titled "Education for the New America," Willard Givens (who will become executive secretary of the NEA in 1935 and serve for seventeen years) says:

> A dying *laissez-faire* must be completely destroyed and all of us, including the "owners," must be subjected to a large degree of social control. . . . An equitable distribution of income will be sought. . . . [And] the major function of the school is the social orientation of the individual. It must seek to give him understanding of the transition to a new social order.

Givens had submitted similar language in the report of the Committee on Education for the New America of the Department of Superintendence of the NEA at the Department's meeting in Cleveland on February 28 of this year.

- *December: NEA Journal* editor Joy Elmer Morgan writes an editorial calling for government control of corporations.

1938

- *June 29:* The *New York Herald Tribune* covering the NEA convention in New York City reports:

> Dr. Goodwin Watson, Professor of Education at Teachers College, Columbia University, begged the teachers of the nation to use their profession to indoctrinate children to overthrow "conservative reactionaries" directing American government and industry. . . . (He) declared that Soviet Russia was one of "the most notable international achievements of our generation."

- *The Purposes of Education in American Democracy* is published by the NEA. In this book, one reads:

> Measurement of outcomes must be directly related to the objectives. . . . Education has, on the whole, been altogether too much concerned with facts, and too little concerned with values. . . . There should be a much greater concern with the development of attitudes, interests, ideals and habits. . . . Our schools should give prizes not to the one who wins more credit for himself, but to the one who cooperates most effectively with

others. . . . The educated citizen is a cooperating member of the world community. . . . Are students becoming more skillful in doing some type of useful work? . . . Are they acquiring skills? . . . Are they learning to be fair and tolerant in situations where conflicts arise? . . . Education is not gained in a few years in school; it is a lifetime enterprise. . . .

It will be worth remembering the quotation above in the latter part of this century, when there will be an emphasis upon outcome-based measurements, values education, cooperative education, school-to-work and skill certificates, teaching tolerance of alternative lifestyles, and lifelong learning. The NEA book quoted above also lists "world citizenship" as an objective of civic responsibility.

1940
- The NEA begins promoting the "Building America" social studies texts, which a California Senate Investigating Committee on Education will later condemn for its subtle support for Marxism or socialism contrary to American values.

1942
- *December: NEA Journal* editor Joy Elmer Morgan writes an editorial, "The United Peoples of the World," in which he quotes Tennyson's "Locksley Hall" with its reference to "the parliament of man, the federation of the world." In his article, Morgan also explains a world organization's or world government's need for an educational branch, a world system of money and credit, a uniform system of weights and measures, a world police force, and other agencies.

1946

- *January:* The *NEA Journal* publishes "The Teacher and World Government" by Joy Elmer Morgan (editor of the *NEA Journal,* 1921–55), in which he proclaims:

> In the struggle to establish an adequate world government, the teacher . . . can do much to prepare the hearts and minds of children for global understanding and cooperation. . . . At the very top of all the agencies which will assure the coming of world government must stand the school, the teacher, and the organized profession.

- *April:* The *NEA Journal* prints "National Education in an International World" by I. L. Kandel of Teachers College, Columbia University, who comments:

> The establishment of the United Nations Education, Cultural and Scientific Organization [sic] marks the culmination of a movement for the creation of an international agency for education which began with Comenius. . . . Nations that become members of UNESCO accordingly assume an obligation to revise the textbooks used in their schools. . . . Each member nation, if it is to carry out the obligations of its membership, has a duty to see to it that nothing in its curriculum, courses of study, and textbooks is contrary to UNESCO's aims.

The NEA played a significant role in UNESCO's founding (see *NEA Today,* February 1993).

- *August:* The NEA sponsors a World Conference of the

Teaching Profession (representatives from twenty-eight nations are present), which drafts a Constitution for a World Organization of the Teaching Profession.

The organization will hold its first regular meeting in August 1947 in Glasgow, Scotland, and will be "a mighty force in aiding UNESCO," in the words of William Carr (associate secretary of the NEA's Education Policies Commission).

1947

▪ *October:* The *NEA Journal* includes "On the Waging of Peace" by NEA official William Carr, who states:

> As you teach about the United Nations, lay the ground for a stronger United Nations by developing in your students a sense of world community. The United Nations should be transformed into a limited world government. The psychological foundations for wider loyalties must be laid. . . . Teach about the various proposals that have been made for strengthening the United Nations and the establishment of world law. Teach those attitudes which will result ultimately in the creation of a world citizenship and world government. . . . We cannot directly teach loyalty to a society that does not yet exist, but we can and should teach those skills and attitudes which will help to create a society in which world citizenship is possible.

In 1928, Carr had authored *Education for World Citizenship*. Late in 1945 he was the deputy secretary for the founding conference of UNESCO in London. And the next year, he founded the World Confederation of Organizations of the Teaching Profession, and acted as its secretary–general until 1970. This is during the same time he will be executive secretary of the NEA from 1952 to 1967. He is also on the board of trustees of the Institute of International Education.

1948

• "Education for International Understanding in American Schools — Suggestions and Recommendations" is produced by the NEA with partial funding by the Carnegie Corporation, and contains the following statements:

> The idea has become established that the preservation of international peace and order may require that force be used to compel a nation to conduct its affairs within the framework of an established world system. The most modern expression of this doctrine of collective security is in the United Nations Charter. . . . Many persons believe that enduring peace cannot be achieved so long as the nation-state system continues as at present constituted. It is a system of international anarchy — a species of jungle warfare. Enduring peace cannot be attained until the nation-states surrender to a world organization the exercise of jurisdiction over those problems with which they have found themselves unable to deal singly in the past.

1952

• The National Training Laboratories (NTL) becomes a part of the NEA. The NTL was founded in 1947 and sponsored by the NEA's Division of Adult Education Service. In 1968 the NTL will separate from the NEA and become an independent organization, and it will later be called the NTL Institute for Applied Behavioral Science (1986).

1956

▪ *November 23:* Former teacher, communist, and organizer of the New York Teachers' Union, Dr. Bella Dodd, states in an interview in the Los Angeles *Tidings:*

> The Communists in the Teachers' Union were for progressive education. We were its most vocal and enthusiastic supporters. I wondered at the time why the people at Columbia (University) were interested in a small union like ours. Then I learned that the function of the Communist Party was to be the lead donkey pulling the drift of American life to the left. Most of the programs we advocated, the National Education Association followed the next year or so. They were following the Columbia group too.

1961

▪ *August 1:* Congressman John Ashbrook enters "International Control of Our Schools" into the *Congressional Record.* He is concerned about the federal education bureaucrats' document "A Federal Education Agency for the Future," which states that the next decade will bring closer relationships with organizations such as UNESCO. He then quotes from a speech by Cardinal James Francis McIntyre, Archbishop of Los Angeles, concerning UNESCO's resolution on "Discrimination in Education," in which the Archbishop states:

> Widespread apprehension that Federal aid to education will socialize American education is confirmed by

the philosophy of this UNESCO resolution passed in Paris in December 1960, and now to be submitted to the Senate. . . . This resolution would substantially eliminate all local control of public education at State or local level. It would place the direction and regulation of all American education under Federal control — control by the U.S. Department of Education and the National Education Association. The resolution would override this Federal control and make it subsidiary to UNESCO as a world court and final international arbiter of education. . . . The policy of the NEA and the U.S. Department of Education, both of which are associated and affiliated with UNESCO, has advocated and sponsored principles in the current legislation for Federal aid to education in the United States that are dishonest and discriminatory. Would it, therefore, not be reasonable to suppose that their competency would be similarly slanted when they would be deciding the circumstances that would entitle non-UNESCO education to recognition? . . .

▪ The NEA's Commission on Professional Rights and Responsibilities lists among its purposes to "gather information about the various individuals and groups who criticize or oppose education, and make resumés of their activities."

▪ In the annual report of the NEA's National Commission for the Defense of Democracy Through Education, one reads:

About one thousand requests for information concerning individuals or groups thought to be causing trouble for the schools or the profession were received during the year. Several new fact sheets and information bulletins concerning critics of education were prepared. The Commission has, probably, the most complete files of their kind of critics of education. [See *Tulsa World* editorial March 27, 1962.]

1962

▪ *Issues in (Human Relations) Training* is published by the National Training Laboratories (of the NEA), and in this book the editors write that human relations or sensitivity training "fits into a context of institutional influence procedures which includes coercive persuasion in the form of thought reform or brainwashing. . . ." The book also includes information about "change-agent skills" and "unfreezing, changing, and refreezing" attitudes. And in David Jenkins' essay in the book, he explains that the laboratories conducted by the NTL have recently moved from an emphasis on skill training to "sensitivity training," and he declares that "the trainer has no alternative but to manipulate; his job is to plan and produce behavior in order to create changes in other people." The manual also states regarding children that although "we appear to behave appropriately . . . this appearance is deceptive. . . . [We are] 'pseudo-healthy' persons who can benefit from sensitivity training."

▪ *April 26:* The *Tulsa Tribune,* after learning that the NEA had a file on its editor under "critics of education," prints an editorial asking: "What is the function of the National Education Association — to improve the education of

America's children or to stifle criticism of present educational methods?"

- *October:* The *Chicago Sun-Times* publishes an editorial stating:

> That the National Education Association . . . advocated Federal aid has surprised us at times. But no longer. For control — real control over the Nation's children — is being shifted rapidly to the NEA. That organization has about completed the job of cartelizing public school education under its own cartel. It is doing so under an organization known as the National Council for Accreditation of Teacher Education, an agency whose governing council is tightly NEA controlled. . . . The manner in which the NEA is usurping parental prerogatives by determining the type of education offered . . . is . . . very simple: control the education and hiring of teachers. . . . NEA has no apprehension regarding Federal control of public schools as a consequence of Federal aid. *It has control itself.* It is extending that control over colleges and universities. In the NEA scheme of things it will be a simple matter to extend control over whatever Washington agency handles the funds. [emphasis added]

- *October 20:* The *New York Times* publishes "McMurrin Insists He Quit to Teach" by Wallace Turner, in which he writes that before Sterling McMurrin resigned as U.S. Commissioner of Education, Dr. McMurrin told NEA head William Carr:

You and I head up the biggest bureaucracies in Washington. NEA has all of the bureaucratic shortcomings and is in danger of moving toward national control of education, not by the Federal Government but by the NEA.

1963

▪ *March/April:* A special supplement of *AV Communication Review* is published as "Monograph No. 2 of the Technological Development Project of the NEA." The project is under contract number SAE-9073 with the U.S. Office of Education of HEW, as authorized under Title VII, Part B, of the National Defense Education Act of 1958. The contractor is the NEA, and in this supplement, one finds:

> Another area of potential development in computer applications is the attitude changing machine. Dr. Bertram Raven in the Psychology Department at the University of California in Los Angeles is in the process of building a computer-based device for changing attitude. This device will work on the principle that students' attitudes can be changed effectively by using the Socratic method of asking an appropriate series of leading questions logically designed to right the balance between appropriate attitudes and those deemed less acceptable.

1966

▪ Arthur Combs becomes president of the NEA's Association for Supervision and Curriculum Development (ASCD). In ASCD's *To Nurture Humaneness: Commitment for the '70s,* Combs will write:

The ASCD Commission on Humanism in Education compiled another list of dehumanizing practices and conditions. In this list were the following: The marking (grading) system, corporal punishment, curricular tracking, teacher evaluation of students, and the single "right" answer syndrome. . . . Vital questions of values, beliefs, feelings, emotions, and human interrelationships in all forms must be integral parts of the curriculum. To achieve this end, it is not enough that we simply teach the humanities. . . . Humanism and the Humanities are by no means synonymous.

1967

- *Humanizing Education: The Person in the Process* is edited by Robert Leeper for the Association for Supervision and Curriculum Development of the NEA, and contains Carl Rogers' article, "The Interpersonal Relationship in the Facilitation of Learning," in which Rogers declares " . . . the goal of education is the facilitation of change. . . . "

Rogers was taught by William H. Kilpatrick at Teachers College where he received his Ph.D. in 1931. As a psychologist, he originated client-centered psychotherapy and helped found (with Abraham Maslow, Rollo May, Ira Progoff, and others) the Association for Humanistic Psychology in 1962.

- *October:* The *NEA Journal* publishes "Helping Children to Clarify Values" by Louis E. Raths, Merrill Harmin, and Sidney B. Simon, in which the authors declare:

Reprinted with permission of *The Gazette*

The old approach seems to be to persuade the child to adopt the "right" values rather than to help him develop a valuing process. . . . Clarifying is an honest attempt to help a student look at his life and to encourage him to think about it in an atmosphere in which positive acceptance exists. . . . The teacher must work to eliminate his own tendencies to moralize.

• *November:* The *NEA Journal* publishes "The 'New' Social Studies," in which one reads:

Probably the most obvious change occurring in the social studies curriculum is a breaking away from the traditional dominance of history, geography, and civics. Materials from the behavioral sciences . . . sociology, social psychology. . . are being incorporated into both elementary and secondary school programs.

• *December:* NEA executive secretary Sam Lambert in the *NEA Journal* comments:

NEA will become a political power second to no other special interest group. . . . NEA will have more and more to say about how a teacher is educated, whether he should be admitted to the profession, and depending on his behavior and ability whether he should stay in the profession.

1968
• Elizabeth Koontz becomes the head of the National Education Association, making "teacher power" the rallying cry of her administration. She advocates that teach-

ers "organize, agitate, and strike." She also promotes the Kibbutz concept. On September 23 she addresses the American Association of Colleges for Teacher Education and states:

> The NEA has a multi-faceted program already directed toward the urban school problem, embracing every phase, from the Headstart Program to sensitivity training for adults — both teachers and parents.

1969

▪ *January: Today's Education* (published by the NEA) contains an article, "Forecast for the '70s," by Harold and June Shane. Their article is a digest of many articles, within which one finds the following comments:

> Ten years hence it should be more accurate to term him [the teacher] a "learning clinician." This title is intended to convey the idea that schools are becoming "clinics" whose purpose is to provide individualized psychosocial "treatment" for the student, thus increasing his value both to himself and to society. . . . Educators will assume a formal responsibility for children when they reach the age of two . . . [with] mandatory foster homes and "boarding schools" for children between ages two and three whose home environment was felt to have a malignant influence, [and children would} become the objects of [bio-chemical] experimentation.

▪ *April: Today's Education/ NEA Journal* publishes Sidney Simon's article, "Down With Grades," in which he proclaims:

For me, the grading system is the most destructive, demeaning, and pointless thing in education. . . . In all candor, the only justification for grades is that they allow certain administrative conveniences. . . . Certainly, grades don't advance learning. . . . What our students get out of a course boils down to a single, crude letter of the alphabet. Let's face up to what grades do to all of us, and banish from the land the cry, "Whatjaget?"

1970

- The Association for Supervision and Curriculum Development (ASCD) of the NEA publishes *To Nurture Humaness: Commitment for the '70s.* There is a disclaimer that the views expressed in the book's essays represent only the views of the authors, but since essayist Raymond Houghton is a member of the ASCD's 1970 Yearbook Committee, it would seem logical that the NEA's ASCD cannot dissociate itself from him entirely. In his essay, Houghton remarks:

There are those who are, on an increasingly sophisticated level, coming to know how behavior is changed. . . . While *absolute* behavior control is imminent, the crucial question concerns itself with identifying the practical critical factor as to when *sufficient* behavior control is accomplished to make the question of *absolute* behavior control only academic. . . . The critical point of behavior control in effect, is sneaking up on mankind without his self-conscious realization that a crisis is at hand. Man will not ever know that it is about to happen. He will never self-consciously know that it has happened.

- *July 3:* NEA president George Fischer tells NEA representatives at an assembly that

> a good deal of work has been done to begin to bring about uniform certification controlled by the unified profession in each state. A model Professional Practices Act has been developed, and work has begun to secure passage of the Act in each state where such legislation is needed. With these new laws, we will finally realize our 113-year-old dream of controlling who enters, who stays in, and who leaves the profession. Once this is done, we can also control the teacher training institutions.

- *September:* In NEA's *Today's Education* editorial, one reads:

> The change-agent teacher does more than dream; he builds, too. He is part of an association of colleagues in his local school system, in his state, and across the country that makes up an interlocking system of change-agent organizations. This kind of system is necessary because changing our society through the evolutionary educational processes requires simultaneous action on three power levels.

1971

- *Rules for Radicals* by socialist Saul Alinsky is published. According to Suzanne Clark in *Blackboard Blackmail*, John Lloyd (executive director, February 1980–June 1984, of the Kansas National Education Association, an NEA affiliate) will say that this book by Alinsky will become the NEA's "bible." In Alinsky's book, which has an "acknowledgment" to Lucifer at the front, he asserts that "any revolutionary change must be preceded by a passive, affirmative, non-challenging attitude toward change among the masses of our people." He continues to say that the radical organizer

> dedicated to changing the life of a particular community must first rub raw the resentments of the people of the community; fan the latent hostilities of many of the people to the point of overt expression. He must search out controversy and issues. . . . An organizer must stir up dissatisfaction and discontent. . . . He knows that all values are relative. . . . Truth to him is relative and changing.

Perhaps not coincidentally, at about this time, HEW lets contract number OEC-0-8-080603-4535 (010) under which portions of *Training for Change Agents* (1973) by Ronald and Mary Havelock will be developed, and in which one reads:

> The Advocator-Organizer-Agitator (ADORAG) and Social Architect change agents would receive training in value clarification. . . . Because of his political and ego strength, the ADORAG is relatively invulnerable to the system. He is able to ride or create a crisis . . . to escalate frictions and protests. . . . Knowledge of the law and strategies of confrontation and civil disobedience will be extremely helpful. . . . Three to six "crucial" school districts in one state would be identified in which

inside and outside change teams would work on their projects.

In the spring of 1974, the federal Office of Education will give a grant of $5.9 million for five hundred "change agents" to be trained at twenty-one institutions of higher education around the country.

• *Schools for the '70s and Beyond: A Call to Action* is published by the NEA, and declares that

> . . . teachers who conform to the traditional institutional mode are out of place. They might find fulfillment as tap-dance instructors, or guards in maximum security prisons or proprietors of reducing salons, or agents of the Federal Bureau of Investigation — but they damage teaching, children, and themselves by staying in the classroom.

• Lifetime NEA member Luther H. Evans becomes the president of World Federalists U.S.A. until 1975. This organization works for the establishment of a world federal government. Evans was director-general of UNESCO from 1953 to 1958.

1972

• NEA president Catherine Barrett states: "We are the biggest potential political fighting force in this country and we are determined to control the direction of American education." (See "A Relic of the New Age: The National Education Association" by Robert Kagan in *The American Spectator,* February 1982.)

1973

• *February 10:* In the same edition of *Saturday Review of Education* that radical feminist leader Gloria Steinem declares "by the year 2000 we will, I hope, raise our children to believe in human potential, not God, . . ." NEA president Catherine Barrett pronounces:

> Dramatic changes in the way we will raise our children in the year 2000 are indicated, particularly in terms of schooling. . . . We will need to recognize that the so-called "basic skills," which currently represent nearly the total effort in elementary schools, will be taught in one-quarter of the present school day. . . . When this happens — and it's near — the teacher can rise to his true calling. More than a dispenser of information, the teacher will be a conveyor of values, a philosopher. . . . We will be agents of change.

1974

• NEA president Helen Wise addresses NEA political fund-raisers and comments: "We must reorder Congressional priorities by reordering Congress. We must defeat those who oppose our goals."

1975

• The NEA Resolutions Committee meets in Washington, D.C., and proposes a resolution that says no person should be "dismissed or demoted because of . . . sexual orientation." This is typical of the radical types of resolutions (on such subjects as abortion-rights) that the NEA will support in future years. These resolutions will also clearly demonstrate the hypocrisy of the NEA, which on the one hand will advocate the right to abortion as a matter of "privacy," but then will support comprehensive sex education which includes a virtual "sexual organ recital" K–12 seemingly ignoring students' "privacy right" not to be exposed to this in a public school classroom with other students (male and female) present.

▪ *November–December: Today's Education* (the NEA's journal) publishes NEA president John Ryor's editorial, "The Uses of Teacher Power," in which he declares: "We must become the foremost political power in the nation."

1976

▪ *February 5:* The *Los Angeles Times* publishes Richard Bergholz' article, "Teachers Group Seeks National System Like Hitler's for U.S. Schools, Reagan Says," in which the future President Reagan says at a Florida rally that the NEA really wants

> a federal educational system. a national school system, so that little Willie's mother would not be able to go down and see the principal or even the school board. She'd actually have to take her case up to Congress in Washington. I believe this is the road to disaster and the end of academic freedom.

▪ The NEA makes available to public schools around the nation a program titled "A Declaration of Interdependence: Education for a Global Community."

▪ *September–October: Today's Education* publishes NEA president John Ryor's editorial, "Education for a Global

Reprinted with permission of *The Gazette*

Community," describing the NEA Bicentennial Committee theme of world interdependence. In the same issue is also published "The Seven Cardinal Principles Revisited" concerning the NEA Bicentennial Committee's work (culminating in the *NEA Bicentennial Ideabook*) regarding "a reframing of the cardinal principles of education (1918) and recommendations for a global curriculum." A report has been prepared by project chairman Harold Shane. In this article, there is material from the report dealing with the seven cardinal principles, including the statement:

> There are striking similarities of thought between the 1918 report and the present Panel's thinking. For one thing, the NEA Bicentennial Panelists emphasized the importance of a global viewpoint. Various statements supported "loyalty to the planet as well as to the nation," the "need for a world view," "world citizenship," and the need for "membership in much larger societies" or for recognizing that "citizenship is more narrow than chauvinism."

The report also said "educators around the world are in a unique position to help bring about a harmoniously interdependent global community."

Terrel H. Bell of the U.S. Office of Education was a member of the NEA's Cardinal Principles Preplanning Committee, and he will be named by President Reagan as U.S. Secretary of Education in 1981.

1978

▪ *November: Reader's Digest* publishes "The NEA: A Washington Lobby Run Rampant" by Eugene Methvin, in which he remarks:

> By the early 1970s, a "Young Turk" faction had gained control of the NEA . . . and launched into full-scale unionism. . . . When Terry Herndon became NEA's executive director in 1973, he set about building a huge political machine. . . . What is the NEA's ultimate goal? Herndon is blunt: "To tap the legal, political, and economic powers of the U.S. Congress. We want leaders and staff with sufficient clout that they may roam the halls of Congress and collect votes to re-order the priorities of the United States of America." [Herndon made these remarks at the NEA convention in July 1978.]

1979

• *February:* The NEA holds its seventeenth annual Conference on Human and Civil Rights in Washington, D.C., and the keynote speaker is Jean Houston talking on "The Rise of the New Right." Houston is a New Ager who is promoted by theosophists, and who will be described in the *San Francisco Chronicle* as a "shaman." She is president of the Association of Humanistic Psychology, and has worked in many countries under the auspices of UNESCO. She calls what she does "priest craft," and believes that each person is "simply God in hiding." She and her sexologist husband, Robert Masters, have developed something called "the Witches' Cradle."

In her keynote address to this NEA conference, she proclaims:

Many of you here, I am certain, have been the occasion for the sudden opening of the minds of children from darkness to illuminist humanity. . . . The moral mandates, . . . the standard brand governments, religions . . . is breaking down. . . . The New Age is seeded and created. . . . And who is it done by? I suggest largely by educators. . . . We are about to become planetary people. . . . We are in an age of frightening interdependence. The old territorial imperatives must give way to the necessities of a mutually shared planet. . . .

■ *October 17:* President Jimmy Carter signs Public Law 96:88 establishing the U.S. Department of Education, despite editorials by the *Washington Post* and many other major daily newspapers indicating there should not be a federal Department of Education (see editorials in the March 7, 1979, *Congressional Record* on pages 4205–11). President Carter, however, had pushed hard for the establishment of the Department as a fulfillment of his campaign promise to the NEA to gain its endorsement of him in 1976.

1980

■ *July 9:* The *Washington Post* prints David Broder's nationally syndicated column in which he describes his interview with NEA executive director Terry Herndon at the union's annual convention. Broder asks about parents' and voters' concern over the poor quality of public schools, and Herndon replies that the convention speakers and delegates "don't know what the answer is. . . . We don't have the answers. Our executive board spent more time talking about the crisis in urban education than any other topic this year, but we have no answer."

1981

- *July 25:* The communist *Daily World* publishes an article in which one reads: "Nowhere in the basic documents of the NEA, in their resolutions or new business items, are there any anti-Soviet or anti-socialist resolutions. This is susceptible to change, of course, if progressive forces are not vigilant."

1982

- The NEA sues Suzanne Clark for her published criticisms of the labor union. She is legally defended by Concerned Women for America, and in her book, *Blackboard Blackmail* (endorsed by Dr. D. James Kennedy), she will later relate that in deposition testimony, then-NEA president Willard McGuire admitted it would be accurate to say the NEA effectively "declared war against the New Right" and the lawsuit reasonably could be characterized as an example of that declaration. Dorothy Massie with the NEA admitted she maintained about twelve file drawers on the "New Right," but on the advice of her attorney, she refused to produce any information from those files. On December 2, 1983, the NEA withdrew its suit against Suzanne Clark. In her book, she quotes Kansas National Education Association executive director John Lloyd as stating that the NEA

> is controlled and run by a group of non-educators . . . well-paid professional staff who have their own agenda, which is not necessarily in the best interests

ic education or of the poorly paid teachers who
lly serve it.

Lloyd is also reported to have revealed that *Rules for Radicals* author Saul Alinsky, hired to train NEA staff members, "integrated radicalism" into the union.

• *January:* The *American School Board Journal* in its "lagniappe" column states:

> Everyone knows it's true, of course, but we prefer to allow the teacher unions to say it in their own words. Notes a bulletin recently sent to teachers from a local chapter of the Oregon Education Association (NEA affiliate): "The major purpose of our associations is not the education of children, rather it is or ought to be the extension and/or preservation of our members' rights. We earnestly care about the kids and learning, but that is secondary to the other goals."

1983

• The NEA distributes "Combatting the New Right," which is a training program developed by the NEA Western States Regional Staff. It criticizes Phyllis Schlafly, Mel and Norma Gabler, Howard Phillips, and other members of the "New Right." The program tells a teacher:

> You are a target of the Far Right [if] you ask students to examine their values, teach sex education, ever indicate it may be okay to lie, teach about values different from those of the students' parents, teach that "any-

thing goes" or, "if you feel it's okay, do it," train your students to be "global citizens," teach humanism, etc.

A number of NEA state affiliates will follow the NEA lead in this area and produce their own publications, such as the Michigan Education Association's "Far Right/Extremist Attacks on Public Education."

• *April 5:* The *Washington Post* editorial, "Political Teaching," accuses the NEA of preparing curriculum materials on nuclear weapons, atomic war, and the American arms build-up, which are "political indoctrination." The curriculum is called "Choices: A Unit on Conflict and Nuclear War."

• *Early June:* John DeMars, director of NEA Peace Programs and International Relations, and Sam Pizzigati, associate director of NEA Communications, travel to Nicaragua and make an on-site report which compares Marxist Nicaragua favorably to El Salvador. Their conclusion states that "the United States should stop its military aid to the Contras" fighting the Marxists in Nicaragua.

• *November 14:* U.S. Senator Steve Symms writes a letter in which he states:

> I am writing you today to alert you to a radical Big Labor takeover of the schools in your community. The National Education Association (NEA) — a union second only to the Teamsters in size and power — is about to seize total control of public education in America. Unless you and I take immediate action on this emer-

gency situation, the NEA will succeed in pushing legislation through Congress that will force compulsory
unionization on every public school in the country. This
is not an idle threat. It is just one part of the NEA's
Legislative Program for the 98th Congress, adopted at
its July 1982 Convention in Los Angeles. Further, the
NEA has publicly boasted of its plan to seize control of
the agencies and boards that decide who is allowed to
teach and what is to be taught. . . . The NEA has become the most powerful special interest group in the
U.S. Their lobbying has brought about a seventeen-fold
increase in federal education spending in the last twen-
ty years. In 1982, their contributions of $1,183,215 and
their army of "volunteer" campaign workers helped
elect 222 Congressmen — a majority of the House of
Representatives. But instead of using its influence to
improve the quality of American education, the NEA
has presided over the virtual crumbling of our nation's
schools."

1983–84

• In the NEA's *Today's Education* 1983–84 Annual Edition, one reads:

The National Education Association believes that communications between certificated personnel and students must be legally privileged. It urges its affiliates
to aid in seeking legislation that provides this privilege
and protects both educators and students.

Parents apparently are not to know what communication
occurs between their children and these educators.

1984

- *NEA: Trojan Horse in American Education* by Samuel Blumenfeld is published, in which he remarks:

> The NEA is probably the most intellectually dishonest organization in America. It is part union, part professional organization, and part political party. Its object is to control the Congress, the fifty state legislatures, the Democratic Party, the curriculum in all the schools, public and private, and the entire teaching profession. Its interest in academics is subordinate to its radical political and social ends. . . . The NEA is as pro-socialist as was John Dewey.

- *Peace and World Order Studies: A Curriculum Guide* (fourth edition) is published and endorsed by the NEA. It is a seven hundred fifty-page curriculum guide published by the World Policy Institute located at 777 United Nations Plaza in New York City.

1986

- One of the resolutions adopted by the NEA Representative Assembly this year is "A-2. Public Education," which states: "Free public schools are of utmost significance in the development of our moral, ethical, spiritual, and cultural values." Since God and Judeo-Christian prayers have been removed from public schools in an official capacity, one can imagine what "spiritual" and "moral" values are being developed.

1987

- The Gay and Lesbian Caucus of the NEA is established.

▪ *June 25:* The communist *People's Daily World* publishes "A Fighting Teachers Union" about the NEA, in which it states:

> The union's progressive policies and united actions indicate that the 1987 convention will continue to provide leadership for its membership and set an example for the labor movement as a whole [see page 15A].

1988

▪ *February 1–5:* The Soviet-American Citizens' Summit (New Age networker Barbara Marx Hubbard is an organizer) is held in Alexandria, Virginia, with a delegation of approximately one hundred Soviets coordinated by the Soviet Peace Committee (SPC). According to a 1985 State Department report on Soviet "Active Measures," the SPC is linked to the Soviet Central Committee's International Department, which was created by Stalin to carry out subversion within other countries. Interesting is the fact that the education task force at the summit recommended that the National Education Association guide a global computer program.

▪ *May 13–16:* Along with the Carnegie Council on Ethics and International Affairs, Foreign Policy Association, Global Tomorrow Coalition, International Development Conference, and others, the NEA co-sponsors the American Forum on Education and International Competence. Some of the workshop topics include: Developing Strategies for Internationalizing State Curriculum; the U.N. University — T en Years of Thinking Globally, Acting Locally; Will They Use It? Implementing Global Education

Initiatives; the United Nations in Global Education; and Political/Religious Challenges to Global Education.

- *July 4 weekend:* At the NEA's annual convention, president Mary Hatwood Futrell states:

> I have decided that the most electable and desirable candidate is Michael Dukakis. . . . Our job is to turn out every one of our 1.9-million members. . . . Fortunately, we have an effective weapon. . . . That weapon is our political power. . . . We have succeeded in building one of the most powerful political networks in the nation. There are literally thousands of organized and motivated NEA members in each congressional district in America.

At its annual convention, the NEA also adopts Resolution C-34 stating:

> The National Education Association believes that home-school programs cannot provide the child with a comprehensive education experience. The Association believes that, if parental preference home-school study occurs, students enrolled must meet all state requirements. Instruction should be by persons who are licensed by the appropriate state education licensure agency, and a curriculum approved by the . . . state department of education should be used.

1990

- *October: NEA Today* prints the comments of Mary Faber (of the NEA's Human and Civil Rights Division) that

"both right-wing and religious extremists have . . . se-
cured bans on textbooks containing stories about violence
and sorcery." And Ms. Faber recommends that teachers
"report 'anti-satanist' activity immediately to your local
[NEA] association. It's your best defense against what's
usually the real aim of such activity — an attack on public education."

1991

▪ Early this year, *The Teachers' Vision of the Future of
Education: A Challenge to the Nation* is printed by Impact II: The Teachers Network. It is praised by NEA president Keith Geiger, and in it one reads that teachers should
be in charge of funds, curriculum, personnel decisions,
and (perhaps) all other educational matters. The report
also recommends that

> rather than narrow nationalism, in our future, we must
> emphasize that we are members of the world commu-
> nity. Therefore, our vision of teacher empowerment
> extends beyond the United States and includes the idea
> of the United League of Teachers, based at the United
> Nations.

▪ NEA president Keith Geiger becomes chairman of the
NEA-originated National Council for Accreditation of
Teacher Education (NCATE), a private standards-setting
board for teacher education programs at about five hundred institutions. Future NEA president Bob Chase will
be chairman of NCATE in 1999–2000. The NEA would
like to restrict National Board for Professional Teaching
Standards certification to graduates of NCATE–accredit-

ed programs. This is all relevant to the October 1962 *Chicago Sun-Times* editorial quoted in this book, and to the 1970 quote by NEA president George Fischer about the NEA "controlling who enters, who stays in, and who leaves the profession."

▪ *March:* NEA Today publishes an interview conducted by NEA staffer Stephanie Weiss with Planned Parenthood president Faye Wattleton, in which the latter expresses her support for school-based distribution of contraceptives and "comprehensive sexuality education" which would begin "well before . . . kindergarten age."

▪ *July 4 weekend:* The NEA holds its annual convention, and one of the New Business Items directs the NEA to develop a curriculum guide for a revived Equal Rights Amendment.

1992
▪ The NEA passes resolutions supporting sex education, abortion and homosexual rights. The NEA has a "Gay and Lesbian Caucus," and spends millions of dollars supporting political candidates. This "labor union" is active in many areas not strictly academically related.

1993
▪ *January 23:* Meeting in Stockholm, the two hundred forty international affiliates of the National Education Association (known as World Confederation of Organizations of the Teaching Profession) and the American Federation of Teachers (known as International Federation of Free Teachers Unions) join to form Education Inter-

national (EI). Former NEA head (and current head of WCOTP) Mary Hatwood Futrell will be the president of EI. This could mean the NEA and the AFT in the U.S. will one day merge and attempt to further their goals of nationalizing American education (e.g., national goals, national tests, national teacher certification, etc.), and then internationalizing Americans' and other nations' education.

• *June 7: Forbes* magazine publishes "The National Extortion Association?" by Peter Brimelow and Leslie Spencer. In this article, sharply critical of the NEA, the authors note that "as the National Education Association has gained in monopoly power, the cost of education has increased while its quality has deteriorated."

• *July 2–5:* At the NEA's annual convention in San Francisco, delegates approve resolutions supporting "multicultural/global education," abortion-rights, and "comprehensive school-based clinics." Resolutions are also passed advocating that teachers "be legally protected from censorship and lawsuits" related to sex education, including education regarding sexual orientation.

Resolution B-1 states that "the NEA supports early childhood education programs in the public schools for children *from birth through age eight*" (emphasis added).

And concerning home schooling, Resolution B-58 indicates that "instruction should be by persons who are licensed by the appropriate state education licensure agency, and a curriculum approved by the state department of education should be used."

President Clinton addresses the delegates and thanks

the NEA for "the gift of our assistant secretary," referring to long-time NEA activist and staffer Sharon Robinson, who has become U.S. Assistant Secretary of Education for the Office of Educational Research and Improvement (OERI), and who sits next to Hillary Rodham Clinton on the front row of the NEA convention. President Clinton goes on to say that he believes his goals for America closely parallel those of the NEA, further stating:

> And I believe that the president of this organization would say we have had the partnership I promised in the campaign in 1992, and we will continue to have it. . . . You and I are joined in a common cause, and I believe we will succeed.

On January 1, 1997, Sharon Robinson will go to work for the Educational Testing Service (ETS). According to *Education Week* (December 4, 1996): "Her newly created job is designed to put data from the National Assessment of Educational Progress and other ETS-designed tests into the hands of policymakers."

▪ December 15: *Education Week* reports that "Debra DeLee, the former director of governmental relations for the NEA, has joined the Democratic National Committee as its executive director."

1994
▪ *February: NEA Today*'s cover story is titled "Are Seniors Public Education's Enemy #1?" It is about senior citizens.

• *The NEA and AFT: Teacher Unions in Power and Politics* by Myron Lieberman (chairman of the Education Policy Institute) and Charlene Haar (president of the Education Policy Institute) is published. Lieberman and Haar (formerly head of her local NEA affiliate in South Dakota) are critical of the NEA, and in 1999 Haar will author *NEA/AFT Membership: The Critical Issues.*

• *Dictatorship of Virtue: Multiculturalism and the Battle for America's Future* by Richard Bernstein is published. He has been a reporter for *Time* magazine and is now a reporter for the *New York Times.* In this book, he writes:

> As long ago as 1973, the National Education Association grandly proclaimed: "All whites are racists. Even if whites are totally free from all conscious racial prejudice, they remain racist, for they receive benefits distributed by a racist society through racist institutions."
> ... The National Education Association ... resolved at its conference in 1991 to call on its members to present an "all-sides analysis of the Columbus landing" to pupils across the nation. "Never again will Christopher Columbus sit on a pedestal in United States history," an explanatory article in the NEA's journal, *NEA Today*, declared. "Christopher Columbus brought slavery to this hemisphere," the article said. "The native American population was reduced from perhaps 60–70 million to a tiny fraction of that as a result of contact with Europeans," it said. ...

1995

• *Freedom on the Altar* by William Norman Grigg is published. The author relates a conversation he had with Gail

Burry, president of the Florida Education Association (NEA affiliate), in which she stated: "We just need to give students all the facts. . . . We can't do this if we're going to start by setting ourselves up as a superior nation."

• *August:* The front-page headline of *The Phyllis Schlafly Report* this month is "The NEA Proves Itself Extremist Again." It is largely about the NEA annual convention over the July 4 weekend and the "extremist resolutions" presented there. The *Report* states:

> The NEA supports socialized medicine (which recognizes "domestic partners" as dependents), statehood for the District of Columbia, gun control, taxpayer benefits to illegal aliens, a national holiday honoring Caesar Chavez, ratification of the U.N. Treaty on the Rights of the Child. . . . The NEA even wants the purpose of Thanksgiving to be changed from thanking God to a celebration of "diversity." . . . The NEA even opposes "competency testing" for the hiring, evaluation, placement, or promotion of teachers.

1996

• *July 4 weekend:* The NEA holds its annual convention, where President Clinton addresses the delegates and receives the NEA's "Friend of Education" award. The president is endorsed for re-election by ninety-one percent of the delegates, which represents a higher approval rating than the entire Democratic Party gives him.

• *August 23:* The *Wall Street Journal* publishes "As Democrats Meet, The Teachers' Unions Will Show Their

Clout" by staff reporters Glenn Burkins and Glenn Simpson, who write:

> When the Democratic convention opens in Chicago Monday afternoon, the raw political power of the teachers' unions will be on display. More than four hundred delegates — roughly one in ten — will be members of the National Education Association. . . . At the national level in 1994, the union's political-action committee donated about $2,250,000. Of that, $2,230,000 went to Democrats. But the numbers vastly understate the NEA's political spending. . . . For example, $3.6 million (of the NEA's annual budget) will go to "support the election of pro-education candidates and ballot measures."

1997

▪ *February 6: Investor's Business Daily* publishes "Is Tide Turning Against The NEA?" by Mike Antonucci, managing editor of *Dispatches,* a publication of the Western Journalism Center. In the article, he indicates that

> the NEA finds itself more and more on the defensive. Here are just a few NEA setbacks over the past year: In April, the 6th U.S. Circuit Court of Appeals ruled teachers who object to the use of their union fees for political purposes are not bound by the union-dominated arbitration process. The decision essentially upholds the right of teachers to bypass union kangaroo courts and file suit. . . . In January this year, the Indiana Court of Appeals abolished the state union's "forced dues" contract. The decision may allow teachers to re-

claim $1 million in illegally demanded dues. Also in January, the National Right to Work Legal Defense Foundation won a ruling that will require the NEA's Pennsylvania affiliate to open its books to objecting teachers. . . . The new light being shed on union activities can only lead to more setbacks for the NEA. . . .

• *July 4 weekend:* The NEA holds its annual convention, during which a choir of young black singers sing two religious songs, one of which is "What a Mighty God We Serve." The following day, NEA president Bob Chase apologizes from the platform for the religious songs having been sung, as he emphasizes they had not been cleared by the NEA. However, a lesbian caucus at the convention promoted a ninety-minute video titled "It's Elementary: Teaching About Gay Issues in School."

Buttons worn at the NEA's 1997 annual convention

• *July:* Kansas Education Watch Network's "Update" states that the following are actual excerpts from a transcript of an audio cassette tape used to train NEA labor negotiators in the Midwest:

In order to apply pressure tactics properly, your negotiating team needs to know and understand your board and its negotiating team thoroughly. Uncovering information about the board, the superintendent and the board negotiating team are critical to your success in negotiations. . . . The suggested data to be gathered on board members is the following: each one's age, the number of years on the board, his education, the organizations he belongs to, . . . and don't forget his religious affiliation. His estimated income and property ownership become very important to you, his employment or occupation; . . . find out about his family; his marital status; the number of children he has and their ages and what schools they go to. And also don't forget to check into his politics. . . . Wear down the board physically and psychologically. . . . Remember to apply pressure tactics on the board team or board members subtly, since open public evidence of the tactics you are using will have the disastrous effect of unifying the board and you don't want that. . . .

▪ *The Teacher Unions* by Myron Lieberman (a former union official) is published, in which he concludes: "The only way to prevent the NEA (and American Federation of Teachers) from spending nonmember fees for unwanted political activities is to prohibit the fees."

1998

▪ *July 25:* Mary Hatwood Futrell (former NEA president) is re-elected president of Education International, whose Elections Committee chairman Keith Geiger (former NEA president) announces the new top officer slate.

▪ *October 7: Education Week* publishes "NEA Report Takes Aim at 'Ultra-Conservative Network' " about a new one hundred forty-four-page NEA report based upon research led by former NEA and Democratic National Committee staff member Robert Watson. The report says that the "Religious Right" is the heart of the conservative network, and that

> choking off NEA funding is not an end in itself. Rather, evidence indicates that the conservative network uses it as a critical step in achieving its broader aims — a state-by-state assault on public education.

The article states that

> included [in the report] are descriptions of right-leaning think tanks, foundations, and politically active religious organizations. The report also provides short biographies of conservative activists and individuals who have contributed to voucher and paycheck-protection campaigns. All the elements are linked together in a two-page flow-chart."

▪ *October 14: Investor's Business Daily* publishes "How Do You Spell Paranoia? N-E-A" by Bob Williams, president of the Evergreen Freedom Foundation in Seattle, Washington. In this article, Williams reveals:

> We looked into claims made by teachers who said their paychecks were being raided illegally to pay for politics. Our investigation revealed that their suspicions were correct. . . . Using our findings, Washington's at-

torney general charged the NEA and its state affiliate, the Washington Education Association, with violating the state's paycheck protection law, money laundering, and failure to report campaign donations.

- *October 23: Jewish World Review* publishes Thomas Sowell's article, "Ed-u-kai-tchun," in which he comments:

> The biggest single obstacle to the improvement of American education is the National Education Association. . . . But the NEA party line is: "The Nation's students today are threatened only by the failure of policymakers to give education the money it deserves." It would be hard for the NEA to tell a bigger lie if they tried. You would risk a hernia if you tried to carry all the studies which show that more money has virtually no effect on the quality of American education. . . . Why are the Democrats so loyal to the NEA? Because the NEA spends vast millions of dollars supporting the Democrats in both state and national election campaigns.

- *October:* Congress passes the Omnibus-spending bill, which includes a permanent repeal of the NEA's property tax exemption on its Washington, D.C., headquarters building. The tax exemption has been worth about $1.1 million per year recently.

1999

- *January 5: Investor's Business Daily* publishes "The NEA's Political Lesson Plan" by staff writer Michael Chapman, in which he explains:

The nation's largest teachers union wants the U.S. to nationalize health care, start a nuclear freeze, adopt national energy policies and pass more gun-control laws. Yet it doesn't want teachers tested or schools privatized. . . . The NEA has long backed a left-wing political agenda. Many of its proposals seem far removed from improving teachers' working conditions. . . . The NEA's political action committee spent $6 million in the '98 election cycle at all levels to push its agenda. . . . In the '96 election cycle, ninety-nine percent of its political action committee donations to candidates went to Democrats.

▪ *May 20: Investor's Business Daily* publishes "Judge Blocks NEA's Political Shell Game" by Ron Nehring, who writes:

In an ongoing suit against the NEA's California affiliate, the California Teachers Association, U.S. District Judge Charles Legge ordered a halt to the collection of all CTA dues at eight Bay area school districts because the union continues to refuse to provide audited financial statements showing just what the CTA bosses are doing with teachers' money. . . . In Washington State, the NEA affiliate was fined $15,000 just last month for refusing to turn over documents subpoenaed in a lawsuit filed on behalf of teachers by the Evergreen Freedom Foundation. Those documents, since turned over, constitute what the trial judge has called a "smoking gun," pointing to the true extent of the union's political activity.

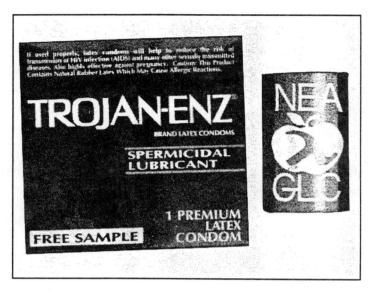

These condoms and NEA Gay & Lesbian Caucus erasers were given away at the NEA's 1999 Annual Convention.

▪ *July 4 weekend:* The NEA holds its annual convention and its president, Bob Chase, in the keynote address proclaims Bill Clinton as "the best education president in history." He goes on to say "forget the media hype coming out of Minnesota," and claims that Lt. Governor Mae Schunk was "having no trouble handling (Governor) Jesse Ventura."

On July 5, Chase presents Hillary Clinton with the NEA's "Friend of Education" award, and he commends her as "an ambassador for education and social justice across the globe." Chase also promotes her book, *It Takes A Village,* as "a rallying cry on behalf of children."

▪ *November 19:* Rush Limbaugh on his national radio program states:

The NEA is not Mrs. Jones [individual teachers].
. . . The NEA is a mob, and it exists for one reason and
that is tenure, to make sure that the most incompe-
tent people never lose their jobs — pure and simple.
And one of the ways they do it is to stay in bed with the
liberal Democratic Party.

▪ *November 23:* Just the Facts Coalition sends a booklet
about sexual orientation and youth to the heads of all
fourteen thousand seven hundred public school districts
in the U.S. The Coalition includes the NEA, and Deanna
Duby of the NEA helped create the booklet, which has
been approved by the NEA's leadership including president Bob Chase. The booklet states:

The idea that homosexuality is a mental disorder or
that the emergence of same-gender sexual desires
among some adolescents is in any way abnormal or
mentally unhealthy has no support among health and
mental health professional organizations. . . . [Repara-
tive] therapy directed specifically at changing sexual
orientation is contraindicated, since it can provoke guilt
and anxiety while having little or no potential for
achieving changes in orientation.

Conservative organizations such as Eagle Forum, Concerned Women for America, the Traditional Values Coalition, and the Family Research Council object that the
booklet is based upon politics and not science.

Concluding Comments

With public education having greatly deteriorated from what it was thirty-five years ago, the American people have noted that the precipitous decline occurred simultaneously with the NEA's rise in political power along with its never ending demand for more money to be spent on education. Parents and others have called for more accountability in education along with a return to the academic basics. Unfortunately, educational leaders usually respond with recommendations for

- site-based management (an end run around locally elected school boards, with power often winding up in the hands of the NEA leader at each site),
- the "new basics" (by which the NEA means much more than traditional academic subjects), and
- outcome-based education (which usually involves shaping students' attitudes, values, or beliefs; which usually costs more; and which allows teachers to avoid accountability by never failing students who they say are simply working at different speeds to reach outcomes).

While it is true that NEA leaders are far more radical than the average teacher who is a member of the NEA, it is important not to forget NEA president George Fischer's remark in 1970 that "we can control the teacher training institutions."

Most teachers who have gone through the training process have had their values "clarified" so that they believe they should not promote the imposition of a particular morality upon their students — and that is the problem! Until about thirty years ago, most teachers believed it was their job to promote the values parents were instilling in their children at home (biblical morality, capitalism over communism, etc.). In buying the "don't impose morality" philosophy, most teachers today apparently do not realize there is no such thing as "value-free" education, and that the non-imposition of a particular morality upon students is itself the imposition of humanistic moral relativism. Even when "honesty" is taught, it is most often not the biblical honesty of moral absolutes, but rather the humanistic honesty of "it's your choice" situation ethics.

The NEA is interested in power and the control of American education, and there is every reason to believe that it will try to control the partially congressionally funded National Board for Professional Teaching Standards, which has been nationally certifying public school teachers, a necessary step toward the nationalization of education under the NEA, and then the internationalization of education under Education International (EI) headed by Mary Hatwood Futrell, former NEA president.

Appendix A

Affective Behavior

by D.L.Cuddy, Ph.D.

For some time, the National Education Association (NEA) has been interested in assessing students' affective behavior (feelings, values, beliefs, etc.). Until 1971 the Association for Supervision and Curriculum Development (ASCD) was a division of the NEA, and in the ASCD's 1962 yearbook (*Perceiving, Behaving, Becoming*), one reads:

> We need to de-emphasize tradition and the past. . . . Educators can no longer deplore and resist change. Too many teachers are still insisting that things be done the "right" way. . . . Messiness, noise, confusions, and mistakes, out of which may come originality, creativity, and genius, are suppressed in favor of neatness, quiet, order, and "being right," out of which can come conservatism, . . . rigidity.

Then, in 1969, the ASCD, NEA published *Improving Ed-*

ucational Assessment & An Inventory of Measures of Affective Behavior, which was the result of an ASCD Council established in May 1965

> in response to concern about the plans of the Exploratory Committee on Assessing the Progress of Education (forerunner of the National Assessment of Educational Progress, NAEP) operating under a grant from the Carnegie Corporation to design a national assessment of the educational attainments of the American people.

In this volume, behavioral psychologist Ralph Tyler (former president of the Carnegie Foundation for the Advancement of Teaching) describes what he considers a need for "diagnosis," which is

> an assessment of the student's environment in order to evaluate his potential success in moving ahead — home environment, language used in the home, types of behavior valued by the student's peer group, and interests and previous experience.

He then talks about his work with the Progressive Education Association (Deweyites) setting educational objectives that

> represented desirable and attainable human outcomes. Now, as the people from [Skinnerian] conditioning have moved into an interest in learning in the schools, the notions of behavioral objectives have become much move specific.

Next, Robert Stake writes that "we seek to serve a plu-
ralistic society. . . . Evaluators should be alert to the fact
that goals are changing. Our world changes. Our needs
change. Our values change." And ASCD council chairman Walcott Beatty asserts that in promoting affective
development, T-groups or sensitivity groups can be used
with

> heavy stress placed on responding to the here and now.
> . . . Group members are encouraged to be experimen-
> tal, to try out feelings and ideas which they might nor-
> mally inhibit in their home situations. . . . We cannot
> leave the development of values to chance.

The last half of the book contains an inventory of measures of affective behavior. There are numerous entries,
including the Pennsylvania Assessment of Creative Ten-
dency which measures such things as "flexible thinking"
and "willingness to take risks." The Interpersonal Orientation Scale assesses "preference levels for manipula-
tive techniques including coercing, evaluating, masking,
coaxing, and postponing. It has been used with school
counselors, teachers, and administrators." The Pennsylvania Citizenship Assessment Instrument questions fifth-
grade students "about their behavior as well as their beliefs." In the Piers-Harris Self-Concept Scale, students
respond "yes" or "no" to statements such as, "My class-
mates make fun of me," and "I cry easily." And, *In the
Way It Looks to Me* (The Ohio State University Delin-
quency Project's Self-Concept Instrument), students respond to questions such as, "Do you think that things are
pretty well stacked against you?" and "Will you probably

be taken to juvenile court sometime?"

If one thinks there are only university projects in assessing students' behavior, the inventory also lists a federal program in Oklahoma City called Children's Self-Concept Scale in which students respond to declarative statements such as, "If I could, I would hurt my friends."

Appendix B

Excerpts of Some Resolutions Passed by the NEA at its 1999 Annual Convention

A-2. **Educational Opportunity for All**

The NEA believes that each student has the right to a free public education that should be suited to the needs of the individual and guaranteed by state constitutions and the U.S. Constitution. Education is a lifelong process, and public schools serve a constituency that embraces all age groups. Access and opportunities for post-secondary education should be widely available, and no qualified student should be denied such opportunities because of the cost of tuition and fees. The Association also believes that all schools must be accredited under uniform standards established by the appropriate agencies in collaboration with the Association and its affiliates.

A-10. **Public School Buildings**

The National Education Association believes that closed public school buildings can be used effectively for public preschool, daycare, job training, and adult education centers. The Association believes that closed public school buildings should be sold or leased only to those organizations that are not in direct competition with public schools.

A-13. **Federal Financial Support for Education**

The Association believes that funding for federal programs should be substantially increased, not merely redistributed among states. The Association further believes that there should be federal support for education whereby:

- The federal government assumes a full partnership role with local school districts by providing significant levels of federal funding for elementary and secondary education
- Federal education funding is clear and identifiable within the federal budget
- Categorical funding is assured in areas such as special education, bilingual/English as a second language, and the economically/educationally disadvantaged.

A-15. **Financial Support of Public Education**

Funds must be provided for programs to alleviate race, gender, and sexual orientation discrimination and to eliminate portrayal of race, gender, and sexual orientation stereotypes in the public schools. The Association opposes the use of public revenues for private, parochial, or other nonpublic pre-K through 12 schools.

A-19. Undocumented Immigrants
The National Education Association believes that, regardless of the immigration status of students or their parents, every student has the right to a free public education in an environment free from harassment.

A-26. Charter and Nontraditional Public School Options
The Association believes that when concepts such as charter schools and other nontraditional school options are proposed, all affected public education employees must be directly involved in the design, implementation, and governance of these programs. The Association further believes that plans should not negatively impact the regular public school program.

A-27. Deleterious Programs
The National Education Association believes that the following programs and practices are detrimental to public education and must be eliminated: privatization, performance contracting, tax credits for tuition to private and parochial schools, voucher plans (or funding formulas that have the same effect as vouchers), planned program budgeting systems (PPBS), and evaluations by private, profit-making groups.

A-29. Voucher Plans and Tuition Tax Credits
The National Education Association believes that voucher plans and tuition tax credits or funding formulas that have the same effect — under which pre-K through 12 nonpublic school education is subsidized by tax monies — undermine public education, reduce the support need-

ﺟ to adequately fund public education, and have the potential for racial, economic, and social segregation of children. The Association opposes all attempts to establish and/or implement such plans.

A-33. Urban Development
The National Education Association believes that professional organizations should be concerned about the quality of life in our cities and should advocate policies or programs concerning land use, zoning, urban development, economic growth, plant closings, mass transit, rent subsidy, or other issues vitally affecting patterns of community development.

B-1. Early Childhood Education
The National Education Association supports early childhood education programs in the public schools for children from birth through age eight. The Association supports a high-quality program of transition from home and/or preschool to the public kindergarten or first grade. The Association further believes that early childhood education programs should include a full continuum of services for parents/guardians/caregivers, and children, including child care, child development, developmentally appropriate and diversity-based curricula, special education, and appropriate bias-free screening devices. The Association believes that federal legislation should be enacted to assist in organizing the implementation of fully funded early childhood education programs offered through the public schools. These programs must be available to all children on an equal basis and should include mandatory kindergarten with compulsory attendance.

B-7. **Diversity**

The National Education Association believes that a diverse society enriches all individuals. Similarities and differences among races, ethnicity, color, national origin, language, geographic location, religion, gender, sexual orientation, age, physical ability, size, occupation, and marital, parental, or economic status form the fabric of a society. The Association also believes that education should increase acceptance and foster an appreciation of the various qualities that pertain to people as individuals or members of a group. The Association further believes in the importance of observances, programs, and curricula that accurately portray and recognize the roles, contributions, cultures, and history of these diverse groups and individuals.

B-8. **Racism, Sexism, and Sexual Orientation Discrimination**

The National Education Association believes in the equality of all individuals. Discrimination and stereotyping based on such factors as race, gender, immigration status, physical disabilities, ethnicity, occupation, and sexual orientation must be eliminated. The Association also believes that plans, activities and programs for education employees, students, parents/guardians/caregivers, and the community should be developed to identify and eliminate discrimination and stereotyping in all educational settings. Such plans, activities, and programs must —

- Increase respect, understanding, acceptance, and sensitivity toward individuals and groups in a diverse society composed of such groups as American Indians/Alaskan natives, Asian and Pacific islanders, blacks, hispanics, women, gays and lesbians, and people with disabilities

- Eliminate discrimination and stereotyping in the curriculum, textbooks, resource and instructional materials, activities, etc.
- Foster the use of nondiscriminatory, nonracist, non-sexist and nonstereotypical language, resources, practices, and activities
- Eliminate institutional discrimination
- Integrate an accurate portrayal of the roles and contributions of all groups throughout history across the curriculum, particularly groups who have been underrepresented historically
- Identify how prejudice, stereotyping, and discrimination have limited the roles and contributions of individuals and groups, and how these limitations have challenged and continue to challenge our society
- Eliminate subtle practices that favor the education of one student over another on the basis of race, ethnicity, gender, physical disabilities, or sexual orientation
- Encourage all members of the educational community to examine assumptions and prejudices that might limit the opportunities and growth of students and education employees
- Offer positive and diverse role models in our society including the recruitment, hiring, and promotion of diverse education employees in our public schools.

The Association encourages its affiliates to develop and implement training programs on these matters.

B-20. **Educational Programs for Limited English Proficiency Students.**

The Association believes that LEP students should be placed in bilingual education programs to receive instruction in their native language from qualified teachers until such time as English proficiency is achieved. The Association values bilingual and multilingual competence and supports programs that assist individuals in attaining and maintaining proficiency in their native language before and after they acquire proficiency in English.

B-33. **Vocational-Technical Education**

The National Education Association believes that preparation of students for vocational-technical jobs should be the responsibility of secondary and higher education in collaboration with labor and business. Vocational-technical education should provide a comprehensive program of lifelong learning for the training, advancement, and promotion of all students.

B-36. **Family Life Education**

The Association believes that programs should be established for both students and parents/guardians/caregivers and supported at all educational levels to promote —
  - The development of self-esteem
  - Education in human growth and development.

The Association also believes that education in these areas must be presented as part of an anti-biased, culturally-sensitive program.

B-37. **Sex Education**

The Association recognizes that the public school must

assume an increasingly important role in providing the instruction. Teachers and health professionals must be qualified to teach in this area and must be legally protected from censorship and lawsuits. The Association also believes that to facilitate the realization of human potential, it is the right of every individual to live in an environment of freely available information and knowledge about sexuality, and [it] encourages affiliates and members to support appropriately established sex education programs. Such programs should include information on sexual abstinence, birth control and family planning, diversity of culture, diversity of sexual orientation, parenting skills, prenatal care, sexually transmitted diseases, incest, sexual abuse, sexual harassment.

B-38. **AIDS Education**

The National Education Association believes that educational institutions should establish comprehensive acquired human immunodeficiency syndrome (AIDS) education programs as an integral part of the school curriculum.

B-40. **Environmental Education**

The Association supports educational programs that promote —

- The concept of the interdependence of humanity and nature
- An awareness of the effects of past, present, and future population growth patterns on world civilization, human survival, and the environment
- The protection of endangered, threatened, and rare species

- Protection of the earth's finite resources
- Solutions to such problems as pollution, global warming, ozone depletion, and acid precipitation and deposition
- The recognition of and participation in such activities as Earth Day, Arbor Day, and Energy Education Day.

B-53. Standardized Testing of Students
The Association opposes the use of standardized tests when —
- Used as the criterion for the reduction or withholding of any educational funding
- Results are used inappropriately to compare students, teachers, programs, schools, communities, and states.

B-65. Home Schooling
The National Education Association believes that home schooling programs cannot provide the student with a comprehensive education experience. When a home schooling occurs, students enrolled must meet all state requirements. Home schooling should be limited to the children of the immediate family, with all expenses being borne by the parents/guardians/caregivers. Instruction should be by persons who are licensed by the appropriate state education licensure agency, and a curriculum approved by the state department of education should be used. The Association also believes that home-schooled students should not participate in any extracurricular activities in the public schools.

First New B. **Racial Diversity Within Student Populations**

The Association believes that a racially diverse student population may not be achieved or maintained in all cases simply by ending discriminatory practices and treating all students equally regardless of race. The Association further believes that, to achieve or maintain racial diversity, it may be necessary for elementary/secondary schools, colleges, and universities to take race into account in making decisions as to student admissions, assignments, and/or transfers.

Second New B. **Assessment of Student Learning**

The National Education Association supports ongoing comprehensive assessment of student growth. The Association believes that the primary purposes of assessment are as follows:

a. To assist students and their parents/guardians/caregivers in identifying the student's strengths and needs
b. To encourage students to become life-long learners
c. To measure a program's effectiveness, communicate learning expectations, and provide a basis for determining instructional strategies
d. To develop appropriate learning experiences for students.

All methods of assessment shall be free of cultural, racial, and gender biases.

C-1. **Health Care for All Children**

The National Education Association believes that legislation should be adopted to provide comprehensive health care to all children.

C-7. Child Care

The Association encourages school districts and educational institutions to establish on-site child care for preschoolers, students, the children of students, and the children of staff members.

C-14. Extremist Groups

The National Education Association condemns the philosophy and practices of extremist groups and urges active opposition to all such movements that are inimical to the ideals of the Association.

C-22. Comprehensive School Health Programs and Services

The National Education Association believes that every child should have direct and confidential access to comprehensive health, social, and psychological programs and services. The Association believes that schools should provide —

- A planned sequential, pre-K through 12 health education curriculum that integrates various health topics (such as drug abuse, violence, universal precautions, and HIV education).

The Association believes that services in the schools should include —

- Counseling programs that provide development alguidance and broad-based interventions and referrals
- Comprehensive school-based, community-funded

student health care clinics that provide basic health care services (which may include diagnosis and treatment)

- If deemed appropriate by local choice, family-planning counseling and access to birth control methods with instruction in their use.

C-23. School Counseling Programs
The National Education Association believes that guidance and counseling programs should be integrated into the entire education system, pre-K through college.

C-31. Suicide Prevention Programs
The National Education Association believes that suicide prevention programs including prevention, intervention, and postvention must be developed and implemented. The Association urges its affiliates to ensure that these programs are an integral part of the school program.

D-20. Testing/Assessment and Teacher Evaluation
The National Education Association believes that competency testing must not be used as a condition of employment, license retention, evaluation, placement, ranking, or promotion of licensed teachers.

E-3. Selection and Challenges of Materials and Teaching Techniques
The Association deplores prepublishing censorship, book–burning crusades, and attempts to ban books from school libraries/ media centers, and school curricula.

E-9. Academic and Professional Freedom
The National Education Association believes that academ-

ic freedom is essential to the teaching profession. Academic freedom includes the rights of teachers and learners to explore and discuss divergent points of view. A teacher shall not be fired, transferred, or removed from his or her position for refusing to suppress the free expression rights of students. The Association further believes that legislation and regulations that mandate or permit the teaching of religious doctrines and/or groups that promote anti-public education agendas violate both student and teacher rights. The Association urges its affiliates to seek repeal of these mandates where they exist.

F-1. Nondiscriminatory Personnel Policies/Affirmative Action

The National Education Association believes that personnel policies and practices must guarantee that no person be employed, retained, paid, dismissed, suspended, demoted, transferred, or retired because of race, color, national origin, cultural diversity, accent, religious beliefs, residence, physical disability, political activities, professional association activity, age, size, marital status, family relationship, gender, or sexual orientation. Affirmative action plans and procedures that will encourage active recruitment and employment of ethnic minorities, women, persons with disabilities, and men in under-represented education categories should be developed and implemented. It may be necessary, therefore, to give preference to men in recruitment, hiring, retention, and promotion policies to overcome past discrimination.

F-37. Employees with HIV/AIDS

The National Education Association believes that education employees shall not be fired, nonrenewed, suspended (with or without pay), transferred, or subjected to any other adverse employment action solely because they have tested positive for the human immunodeficiency virus / acquired immunodeficiency syndrome (HIV/AIDS) antibody or have been diagnosed as having HIV/AIDS.

H-1. **The Education Employee as a Citizen**
The Association urges its members to become politically involved and to support the political action committees of the Association and its affiliates.

H-7. **National Health Care Policy**
The Association supports the adoption of a single-payer health care plan for all residents of the United States, its territories, and the Commonwealth of Puerto Rico. The Association will support health care reform measures that move the United States closer to this goal.

I-1. **Peace and International Relations**
The Association urges all nations to develop treaties and disarmament agreements that reduce the possibility of war, provide for the peaceful resolution of conflicts, and guarantee the rights of nations to coexist within safe and secure borders. The Association also believes that such treaties and agreements should prevent the placement of weapons in outer space. The Association further believes that the United Nations (U.N.) can further world peace and promote the rights of all people by preventing war, racism, and genocide.

I-3. **International Court of Justice**
The National Education Association recognizes that the

International Court of Justice is one instrument to re-
solve international disputes peacefully. The Association
urges participation by the United States in deliberations
before the court.

I-13. Family Planning

The National Education Association supports family planning, including the right to reproductive freedom. The
Association further urges the implementation of community–operated, school-based family planning clinics that
will provide intensive counseling by trained personnel.

I-27. Freedom of Religion

The Association opposes the imposition of sectarian practices in the public school. The Association also opposes
any federal legislation or mandate that would require
school districts to schedule a moment of silence.

I-29. Gun-free Schools and the Regulation of Deadly Weapons

The Association believes that strict proscriptive regulations are necessary for the manufacture, importation, distribution, sale, and resale of handguns and ammunition
magazines.

I-43. Hate-Motivated Violence

The National Education Association believes that hate-
motivated violence against individuals or groups because
of their race, color, national origin, religion, gender, sexual orientation, age, disability, size, marital status, or economic condition is deplorable.

I-47. **English as the Official Language**
The Association believes that efforts to legislate English as the official language disregard cultural pluralism; deprive those in need of education, social services, and employment; and must be challenged.

I-50. **Equal Opportunity for Women**
The Association supports an amendment to the U.S. Constitution (such as the Equal Rights Amendment) that guarantees that equality of rights under the law shall not be denied or abridged by the United States or by any state because of gender.

—Source: *Education Reporter,* August 1999.